The Healing POWER of Joy

TWENTY THIRD 23rd
PUBLICATIONS

Twenty-Third Publications
A Division of Bayard
One Montauk Avenue, Suite 200
New London, CT 06320
(860) 437-3012 or (800) 321-0411
www.twentythirdpublications.com
ISBN:1-58595-536-1

The Scripture passages contained herein are from the *New Revised
Standard Version of the Bible*, copyright ©1989, by the Division of
Christian Education of the National Council of Churches in the U.S.A.
All rights reserved.

Library of Congress Catalog Card Number: 2005929699
Printed in the U.S.A.

Contents

We all want to be happy. This is one desire we certainly have in common. So why are only a few of us truly happy? Are you one of these few? And how happy are you?

We often wonder why some people seem to possess the secret of inner happiness and why they are able to radiate a deep joy in any circumstance. We wonder why others seem bored with life, dispirited, and worried about everything, even when things are going well for them. We also wonder why still others, when they reach a moment of achievement, shout out, "Is this it? Is this all there is?"

We live in a high-risk, crazy society—a world in which unhappiness seems to be the norm. Nervous breakdowns, suicides, broken homes, drug addiction, alcoholism, a variety of crimes and forms of violence, as well as profound unrest and bitter loneliness, are the hallmarks of our time. In addition, we have such individual concerns as our children's welfare, high taxes, overdue bills, poor health, aging, and dying.

To counterbalance all this and to cover up our unbearable dissatisfaction with life, we spend billions on new homes, new cars, high-tech devices, vacations in distant lands, new clothes, unnecessary foods, sporting events, and other forms of entertainment. We think that all these material things will fill the huge holes in our hearts and make us happy. Yet we continue to search for the panacea that we cannot find. None of these worldly pleasures help us attain the inner contentment that has the power to turn everything around.

When we realize the depth of the hole in our hearts and souls, we also realize that only God can fill it. St. Augustine was right when he wrote in his famous *Confessions*, "O Lord, you have made us for yourself, and our hearts are restless until they rest in you."

Happiness is part of human nature. People from every ethnic, cultural, and religious background want it, talk about it, and are eager to have it. We invest more time in schools, we search for better careers, and we get married and raise a family—to be happy. We travel, we vacation, and we connect with others—to be happy. We make plans, we dream for more of everything, and we prudently prepare for retirement—to be happy.

> Spreading real joy is the holiest way to live our lives.

The desire for happiness is the driving force behind the pursuit of everything and anything. In fact, it has been the quest of different civilizations and cultures for centuries. Some thinkers find happiness in peace of mind, others in utopia, some in enlightenment, and still others in the promises of self-knowledge. But is happiness a goal to achieve, or something to feel or possess? When is happiness different from joy? Is "feeling good" the same as living a good life? And, for that matter, do we know who or what makes us live the way we live? Do we know where we are coming from and where we are heading?

I hope you will find in this little book, which is part of "The Healing Power" series, the insight, the inspiration, and the necessary tools to help you answer such questions and live a truly joyful life in all circumstances. This goal is reachable if you know and practice what Augustine refers to, "There is a joy that is not given to those who do not love you (O God), but only to those who love you for your own sake. You, yourself, are their joy."

I also hope that, together, we can learn to love one another more deeply, to sit under a tree, to read, to hit a ball, to listen to silence, to share misfortune and joy, and to smile through tears—one smile at a time. One smile at a time makes our earth more homey, our lives more livable and enjoyable, and the kingdom of God more accessible.

Spreading real joy, especially in a troubled world, is the healthiest, wisest, and holiest way to live our lives.

CHAPTER ONE

More than Just Happy

"Rejoice always."

■ 1 THESSALONIANS 5:16

Unless some mental illness invades our minds, we have to admit that happiness is the overwhelming force that drives our lives.

We were created to be happy. God wants us to be happy. The purpose of our lives is to be happy. By nature we crave happiness and joy. According to St. Thomas Aquinas, we desire happiness naturally and by necessity. "By nature the creature

endowed with reason wishes to be happy," and "To desire to be happy is not a matter of free choice." Originally, we were created to live happily ever after. "The pursuit of happiness," along with "life" and "liberty," was considered an inalienable right by the founding fathers of America. We crave happiness; it is our right, and we pursue it with all our power.

If by nature we are supposed to be happy, why very often are we not?

How Happy Are You?

Are you happy—really happy? Find out through this quiz. Place a number, from 0 to 10 after the following sentences (0 for "strongly disagree," 10 for "strongly agree," and the rest in between).

1. I am completely satisfied with my life._____
2. If I could live all over again, I would change nothing._____
3. I have time to take care of myself._____
4. I have time to take care of others._____
5. I have survived very difficult times._____
6. Bad luck and circumstances do not overwhelm me._____

7. My life has purpose and meaning._____

8. When I think about people, I focus on love, not on hate or indifference._____

9. So far I have achieved all I had in mind to achieve._____

10. I don't care about what others say about me._____

11. To be physically, emotionally, and spiritually fit is very important to me._____

12. I am known as a person others can count on._____

13. My family and friends come first._____

14. Expansive living (i.e. living large or magnificently) does not impress me._____

15. I am concerned with social issues._____

16. I forgive those who hurt me._____

17. I am happy in spite of my stressful circumstances._____

18. I have a real thirst for knowledge._____

19. I try to do good even when I am not thanked._____

20. I pray that I'll always be on God's side._____

The higher your score, the happier you are. I hope you did very well. Besides informing you whether or not you are a happy person, this quiz also has the advantage of revealing to you the source of your happiness and what your values are in life. In addition, it makes you more aware of the difference between "pseudo happiness" and true happiness, or joy.

Pseudo Happiness

There are no short cuts to real happiness. On the other hand, pseudo happiness can be reached quickly. We think we are happy for a while but then a feeling of emptiness takes over, along with sometimes catastrophic consequences.

A typical example of this is addiction to drugs or alcohol or any other addiction for that matter. When consumed by this or that addiction, we might feel a kind of wild excitement, but this is soon followed by deterioration. The accompanying loss of judgment and intellectual keenness often end in depression. The charming euphoria was just pseudo happiness and an ephemeral illusion of contentment.

Another type of pseudo happiness comes from strong emotional moods that often follow depression in people who are bipolar. There is no rational way to explain what causes these unexpected waves. Disease or addiction can never lead to real happiness. Under certain conditions, people can forget their unhappiness for a while, but forgetfulness is not happiness.

Even great feelings of bliss and elation—often in a prophetic person—can occur in a progressive phase of psychosis. Writer Gérard de Nerval (1808–1855), who was known for having schizophrenic characteristics and periodic insanity, describes himself this way: "I felt as if I knew everything and everything was revealed to me, all the secrets of this world I understood in these blissful hours." Philosopher Karl Jaspers (1883–1969) reported that someone once said to him: "I woke up one morning with the most wonderful feeling of being reborn. What blessed delight I felt, what an overwhelming sensation of being freed from everything that is earthly." But these feelings, too, were pseudo happiness.

Happiness does not stem from wealth and notoriety. John Henry Cardinal Newman describes this very well:

> All bow down before wealth. People pay an instinctive homage to wealth. They measure happiness by wealth; and by wealth they measure respectability….It is a homage resulting from a

profound faith…that with wealth they may do all things. Wealth is one idol of the day and notoriety is a second….Notoriety, or the making of a noise in the world—it may be called "newspaper fame"—has come to be considered a great good in itself, and a ground of veneration.

Happiness is not the by-product of the "always more" philosophy—more money, more comfort, more sexual freedom, more thrills, even more religious experiences. "Wanting-ever-more" never satisfied anyone. Those who practice this kind of philosophy are in fact unhappy people because they are always dissatisfied by definition and always want more. Go and ask someone who went on an expensive vacation, built a beautiful house, or bought a luxury car. He or she will tell you without hesitation that happiness lasted for a while, but this was not "it."

Happiness depends more on who we are than what we have.

Think about all the progress we've made since World War II. Our income has probably tripled. The size of our houses has at least doubled. Each family has, in general, two cars if not more. Rare are those who do not have high-tech devices. Spending is up and up and up. But nowhere can we say that happiness has increased at the same time and same pace. Instead, depression seems to have increased and remarkably so; one in fifteen Americans experience episodes of major depression. This is what a recent study, conducted by Ronald Kessler of Harvard Medical School, has found. Money cannot buy happiness. The things that really matter in life are not sold in supermarkets. Daniel Kahneman of Princeton University observed, "Circumstances don't seem to have much effect on happiness."

Happiness is not just having fun either, or indulging in pleasure, or a feeling of mere satisfaction. Happiness seems to lie outside what can be limited, measured, counted, and felt. It is beyond the realm of material wealth and life events. It depends on who we really are, more than it depends on what we have. This is where joy comes in.

What Is Joy?

To focus solely on pleasure resulting from fortunate circumstances is to miss out on many other aspects of what it means to be human—truly human. Doing the right thing is a very good ideal, but being the right person is by far more important.

A personal transformation at the deepest level is required. This is where joy comes in, for it depends on who we are, not on what our circumstances are, or on what we have. Indeed, this could be an important difference between happiness, which comes usually from outside in, and joy or true happiness, which arises from the inside out.

Joy is a fruit of the Holy Spirit, not of our circumstances. Joy is a deep well inside us that waters, animates, and refreshes the events of our lives. Happiness may vanish but joy remains. Bubbly people, who giggle all the time and who seem to have all the fun they want, may or may not have real joy; but those who experience real joy know how to have a calm delight regardless of what is occurring to them and around them. They do not need to wait until they finish school, go back to school, lose a few pounds, get married, have kids, buy a new house or a better car, next year or the year after. They are joyful right now; there is no better time than now because the moment is the only time they have. Alfred d'Sousa was right when he said:

> For a long time it had seemed to me that life was about to begin, real life, but there was always some obstacle in the way, something to be gotten through first. Unfinished business, time still

to be served, a debt to be paid, then life will begin. At last it dawned on me that these obstacles were my life.

Think about this. How true it is!

The achievements and external trappings of success—money, power, possessions, and pleasure—convey the illusion of ultimate satisfaction. They show the real nature of our social and cultural disease that no pill or vaccine can prevent or eliminate. They show that the very things that bring us a delightful satisfaction carry in them the potential for loss and disappointment. They show that joy does not spring from doing and having, but from being.

> Joy is a deep well inside us that waters our lives.

When you are who and what you really are, you cannot help but sparkle with energy and delight. It is in the very center of our being that the fullness of life and joy resides.

There is a large industry of "happiology" out there. Books, articles, and many other tools sketch guidelines for bringing happiness to our lives. Even clubs for laughter have been created. But, in spite of all this, we have to admit that no quick formula for joy has been successful. Digging deep in the center of our being is the way to reach God and the source of our joy. Henri J. M. Nouwen wrote:

> Joy is not the same as happiness. We can be unhappy about many things, but joy can still be there because it comes from the knowledge of God's love for us. We are inclined to think that when we are sad we cannot be glad, but in the life of a God-centered person, sorrow and joy can exist together…. Joy does not simply happen to us. We have to choose joy and keep choosing it every day. It is a choice based on the knowledge that we belong to God and have found in God our refuge and our safety and that nothing, not even death, can take God away from us.

Joy Blockers

Obviously, external circumstances can make our joy more or less tangible. Deadlines, demands of job, family, groups to which we belong, and unexpected unfortunate events are examples of that reality. But there are also interior blocks to joy that deserve our considerate reflection. Take a look at some of them and identify the one(s) that seem(s) relevant to you.

Lack of self-knowledge. The part of your personality that you do not really know may create a problem to your happiness. It is difficult to have real joy when you still have unresolved issues you do not even know exist.

Guilt. It is normal to feel a sense of guilt after wrongdoing. However, when unbalanced, guilt has the potential to evolve into an unreasonable self-blaming, "neurotic" guilt that attracts the need for continuous self-punishment. This can take the form of an accident, illness, or depression. At an unconscious level, people who have this kind of guilt do not really want forgiveness from God and others. They seem to believe that the restoration of their joy will come only through self-punishment. Some people feel guilty after any personal gratification or even just a little innocent fun. Others think they do not deserve personal gratification, or they process it as an either/or possibility. Morbid guilt cannot be a good partner for joy.

Self-criticism. How can you have joy if you keep hammering yourself for anything you do or do not

> "In the life of a God-centered person, sorrow and joy can exist together."
> — Henri Nouwen

do, or for what you are or are not? Succumbing to negative self-evaluation and poor self-esteem does not breed joy.

Fear. The one who lives in constant fear cannot experience happiness because fear and anxiety distort reality, generate confusing thoughts, and paralyze the will. The person in fear often does not know why he or she is fearful. No specific reason can be named, but such symptoms as headaches, indigestion, stomach aches, and distress may appear. When someone does not go forward because of the fear of failure, or the fear of success, he or she is stuck in a debilitating and joyless situation.

Need to control. Some types of control are good when we need to insure security, take steps for progress, and make changes. But the type of control that results from deep anxiety and fear puts the controlling person under continuous stress and denies him or her any real joy.

Mental laziness. When you no longer have new ideas, when nothing new inspires you, and when you lose any sense of creativity, boredom will dismantle your energy, stealing your joy little by little.

Rigid self-image. Most of us, if not all of us, tend to create a certain self-image and a persona with which we like to identify. Celebrities even hire publicists to promote these images for them. Momentum is built on the accumulation of these images. But life is not as clear-cut as the images built over time. When cracks in rigid self-images appear, frustration and depression follow, and joy vanishes.

Perfectionism. In spite of its good, idealistic approach, perfectionism, especially when pushed to the extreme, denies us any true joy. Unrealistic expectations can poison our lives. Who can be perfect? Why do we expect perfection from another if we, ourselves, are not perfect? Perfection should not be a measure of how successful we are, but, rather, of how loving we are. This difference is the key to joy.

Fatigue. Fatigue becomes the enemy of joy when it depletes the energy needed for happy living, and when it makes a person irritable, intolerant, and impatient. Fatigue can take many forms. It can be physical, emotional, or even spiritual. We should never underestimate the value of taking time just to relax and have a dose of good and healthy fun.

Vain regret. The "if only" litany of the past is basically wasteful, paralyzing, and selfish, and it can constitute a serious blow to the pursuit of real happiness. That we should learn from the past is obviously true and wise. To be morbidly preoccupied with, and obsessed by, past failures is another matter. A healthier approach is to leave the matter of judgment to God.

Selfishness. Check your memory. Have you ever met a selfish person who was really happy? I haven't. How can a selfish person be happy when what he or she really wants is be the center of the universe, seeking his or her own pleasure and glorification? Selfishness leads only to unhappiness.

Anger. Anger is bad for you. Besides its capacity to destroy others, unchecked anger can be harmful to your body systems. It can cause high blood pressure, ulcers, headaches, and premature artery disease. I am referring to anger as a negative emotion, not anger that is "righteous" and that motivates a worthwhile cause like a campaign against injustice or violence or poverty, for example. When anger is a negative force, it is a formidable destroyer of joy.

Approval seeking. Our society encourages approval seeking in a big way. Advertisers, experts, and celebrities tend to influence our culture today. If someone else's opinion of you and of what you are supposed to be or to do becomes more important to you than your own inner voice, you will lose your sense of creativity and personal power. Consequently, your capacity for joy will diminish substantially.

Obsession with comparisons. When we are obsessed with comparing ourselves with others, chances for real joy will continue to decline significantly. Indeed, there will always be someone who has more money, more power, more prestige, and more "anything" than us. It is wiser to ask ourselves questions such as "Does my house meet my needs?" instead of "Is my house bigger and nicer than my neighbor's?"

Loss of values. We need ideals, causes, and goals to motivate us. We need strong principles by which to live. We can find great joy in the commitment to spiritual values that transform our lives and the world. Without values, our lives are meaningless and joyless.

Disconnection. Interconnectedness is part of the definition of human nature. Serene connections bring joy. The deepest connection of all is the connection we have with others and with God, which is based on being children of God.

Sin. We are sinners. However, unconfessed sin poisons our lives and robs us of joy. With sin, we lose freedom, for "everyone who commits sin is a slave of sin" (Jn 8:34), and we lose God's blessing, "Your sins have deprived you of good" (Jer 5:25). But God knows, cares, and forgives. "If we confess our sins,

God who is faithful and just will forgive us our sins and cleanse us." (1 Jn 1:9). An unhealthy sense of sin and guilt with the unwillingness to confess and repent is a serious obstacle to joy in our lives.

Happiness is one thing and joy is another. Although they often tend to indicate the same reality, it is important to know the difference between happiness and joy. It is also important to know how to reach true happiness and what to avoid in the process. One recommended tool is self-examination, which shows us things we want to see (our positive traits), as well as things we may not want to see (our personality flaws). Our flaws may be difficult to acknowledge, but how can we reach our potential and realize the fullness of life if we ignore the truth? Real joy does not come unless we are ready for such reflection.

FOR YOUR REFLECTION & RESPONSE

1. Make a list of activities that affirm what you consider essential in your life. Are you pursuing these activities? If not, what is hindering you? Do you feel that you deserve joy? Does what you love to do express your highest vision and purpose in life? Are you guided by your inner voice? Do you trust this inner voice? Describe one situation in which your choice seemed unclear and another situation in which you felt called. Which situation gave you more joy?

2. Finish this sentence: "Finding my joy means…." Write down a five-line answer. Revise it again and again. See how your idea of joy evolves according to a better understanding of your values. Is your answer influenced by past experiences? Did a person or event in your life affect you deeply? Did a future goal play a significant role in what you just wrote?

3. When you ask yourself, "Am I happy?" what instantly comes to your mind? Watch and describe your thoughts, satisfactions, and frustrations. What is your response when you ask

yourself this second question, "Do I deserve to be happy?" Then, ask yourself this third question, "If circumstances make me happy, what do I want more than anything?" Finally, take one step further, "Am I happy no matter what?"

4. Are you a perpetual student for truth? Do you cultivate a deep understanding and continuous search for integrity, clarity, and authenticity? In the midst of changing circumstances, do you look for the rainbow after the rain and the cup that is half full versus half empty? Do you stop to smell the flowers? Do you celebrate your world with laughter and joy no matter what? From where does this deep joy come?

5. Are you struggling with a problem at the present time? Does this problem put you under stress? Does your past control you? Do others' reactions control your choices? Do you have a tendency to postpone living your life? If joy is your goal, do you consider yourself following the road toward that goal?

6. Do you appreciate who you are, what you have, and the way you live your life? Are you aware of your talents and uniqueness? Do you

experience moments of deep joy? Are you able, when things are not working well for you, to turn things around and create the joy your heart desires? How do you handle adversities and frustrations? Do you feel you are open to new experiences and horizons? Is contributing to the joy of others a joy for you?

AFFIRMATION

Repeat this several times a day.

I am awakening
to my potential and
witnessing God's gifts
blossoming in me.

PRAYER

Dear God,

Why am I so irritable?

Sometimes, I feel stressed out and worried. At other times, I feel tired and lack the desire to do anything. At still other times, I feel guilty, frustrated, and angry.

Not that I don't have what I want, for I have a house, a car, a job, and most of what my heart desires: a good family, comfort, and "the good life."

But I don't have what I really need. I don't have contentment and deep joy.

I know now that deep joy does not come from what I own or what I achieve.

Deep joy comes from within, through awareness and contemplation—the kind of water you proposed to the Samaritan woman so that she would never be thirsty again (see Jn 4:7–15).

Dear God, "Give me this water, so that I may never be thirsty" (Jn 4:15) again. Give me your healing joy. Amen.

CHAPTER TWO

Unceasing Joy

"I have said these things to you so that my joy may be in you, and that your joy may be complete."

■ JOHN 15:11

The life of a Christian is defined by a relationship with Christ—the promise of fulfillment. The secret of Jesus Christ was his inner peace despite his suffering and his inner joy in following his Father's will. The secret of our joy is Jesus Christ.

Why did Jesus have inner joy? It is because of his unique relationship with God the Father. He said: "All things have

25

been handed over to me by my Father; and no one knows the Son except the Father, and no one knows the Father except the Son, and anyone to whom the Son chooses to reveal him" (Mt 11:27).

Mark sketched Jesus' message this way: "Now after John was arrested, Jesus came to Galilee, proclaiming the good news, and saying, 'The time is fulfilled, and the kingdom of God is near; repent, and believe in the good news'" (Mk 1:14–15). In the synagogue of Nazareth, Jesus read the scroll: "The Spirit of the Lord is upon me, because he has anointed me to bring good news to the poor" (Lk 4:18). In Jesus, the promises of the Old Testament and the prophecies are fulfilled. He is the Good News that brings joy, peace, and hope.

But what was the foundation of Jesus' joy? What was the secret of this joyful man, who loved life and wasn't afraid of the cross? How could he claim a fullness of life even in the midst of his suffering and death?

As I wrote in my book *Pathways: Finding God in the Present Moment*, "His secret was that he was wrapped at all times in his Father's loving presence. Jesus' delight was to do the will of the Father, and every person and every event were opportunities for him to encounter his Father in the human context and return his love to his Father. This is how he was able to maintain a joyful openness to the fullness of life, even in his suffering."

In the depth of his heart and innermost consciousness—at the very center of his being—Jesus was in continuous touch with the Father. He breathed, smiled, laughed, cried, taught, connected with others, relaxed in nature, and performed miracles in the infinitely holy and loving presence of his Father. This filled him with deep joy, and he generously radiated this joy; he set hearts afire. Jesus drew a road map for this joy, as recorded in Matthew's gospel.

Blessed are the poor in spirit, for theirs is the kingdom of heaven.

Blessed are those who mourn, for they will be comforted.

Blessed are the meek, for they will inherit the earth.

Blessed are those who hunger and thirst for righteousness, for they will be filled.

Blessed are the merciful, for they will receive mercy.

Blessed are the pure of heart, for they will see God.

Blessed are the peacemakers, for they will be called children of God.

Blessed are those who are persecuted for righteousness' sake, for theirs is the kingdom of heaven.

Blessed are you when people revile you and persecute you and utter all kinds of evil against you falsely on my account. Rejoice and be glad, for your reward is great in heaven. (Mt 5:3–12)

If we replace the word "blessed" by the word "happy," as some translations do, we will realize that true happiness or joy, according to Jesus, comes about when we surrender to God's truths, turning away from that what our ego and culture prescribe for happiness.

These beatitudes point directly to the true self—the self in God. Only at this level can a truly happy life exists: "Let all who take refuge in you rejoice; let them ever sing for joy" (Ps 5:11). "Happy are the people whose God is the Lord" (Ps 144:15).

The beatitudes point the way to our well-being and blessing. They do it in poetic, beautiful, and paradoxical sayings. They are counter-cultural because they turn upside down all that we have learned about happiness, correcting our misconceptions, and challenging our lifestyles. They communicate the secret of real joy, which is based on true relationship with God and not on injunctions, prescriptions, and prohibitions. Jesus wanted much, much more than external "righteousness." As he said, "I am coming to you, and I speak these things in the world so that they may have my joy made complete in themselves" (Jn 17:13). "I have said these things to you so that my joy may be in you, and that your joy may be complete" (Jn 15:11).

> "Rejoice and be glad, for your reward is great in heaven."
> (Mt 5:12)

No wonder St. Paul, in spite of his many frustrating experiences and captivity, appears to be the champion and messenger of joy. If, as he wrote, "For me living is Christ and dying is gain" (Phil 1:21), he can keep his joy even when he is in jail, when he is flogged, or when he is exposed to multiple dangers. Circumstances are irrelevant, he seems to be saying, because the joy of God has nothing to do with circumstances. He goes on to say to the Christians of Philippi in crystal clear terms: "Rejoice in the Lord always; again I will say, Rejoice" (Phil 4:4).

> "A joyful heart is life itself...."
> (Sir 30:22)

This insistence of St. Paul on rejoicing is intriguing and, at the same time, adds more credibility to what he is saying. You would have expected this recommendation to come from someone living in comfort and good health, not from someone whose circumstances and conditions were very difficult. What makes all the difference is the phrase "in the Lord." These words give the followers of Christ a reason to rejoice even when they are hungry, thirsty, tired, in pain, isolated, imprisoned, persecuted, or victimized. They rejoice, even in these trials, because they believe that the mighty Lord is always near.

Indeed, rejoice.In any circumstance, rejoice because "the Lord is near" (Phil 4:5).

In the face of difficulties, here are some strategies for joy.

Adversity. "In the world, you face persecution. But take courage; I have conquered the world" (Jn 16:33).

Temptation. "My brothers and sisters, whenever you face trials of any kind, consider it nothing but joy, because you know that the testing of your faith produces endurance" (Jas 1:2–3).

Weakness. "I am content with weaknesses, insults, hardships, persecutions, and calamities for the sake of Christ; for whenever I am weak, then I am strong" (2 Cor 12:10).

Neediness. "Until now you have not asked for anything in my name. Ask and you will receive, so that your joy may be complete" (Jn 16:24).

Sorrow. "Remove sorrow from you, for sorrow has destroyed many and no advantage ever comes from it" (Sir 30:23).

Distress. "Do not distress yourself deliberately. A joyful heart is life itself, and rejoicing lengthens one's life span" (Sir 30:21–22).

Grief. "I will turn their mourning into joy, I will comfort them, and give them gladness for sorrow" (Jer 31:13).

Weeping. "Weeping may linger for the night, but joy comes with the morning" (Ps 30:5).

Health problems. "You shall see, and your heart shall rejoice; your bodies shall flourish like the grass; and it shall be known that the hand of the Lord is with his servants" (Isa 66:14). "A cheerful heart is good medicine" (Prov 17:22).

Pain. "You will have pain, but your pain will turn into joy.... You have pain now; but I will see you again, and your hearts will rejoice, and no one will take your joy from you" (Jn 16:20, 22).

Powerfulness. "Do not rejoice at this, that the spirits submit to you, but rejoice that your names are written in heaven" (Lk 10:20).

Confusion. "Your decrees are my heritage forever; they are the joy of my heart….Your commandments are my delight" (Ps 119:111, 143).

Wrongdoing. "It (love) does not rejoice in wrongdoing, but rejoices in the truth" (1 Cor 13:6). "Happy are those who observe justice, who do right at all times" (Ps 106:3).

Hunger for God's presence. "Sing and rejoice, O daughter of Zion! For lo, I will come and dwell in your midst, says the Lord" (Zech 2:10).

Persecution for being a child of God. "Blessed are you when people hate you, and when they exclude you, revile you, and defame you on the account of the Son of Man. Rejoice in that day and leap for joy, for surely your reward is great in heaven" (Lk 6:22–23).

All this leads to the conclusion that our joy is found by making God our focus; wherever God is, true joy is also. St. Augustine said:

There is joy which is not given to the ungodly, but to those who love thee for thine own sake, whose joy thou thyself art. And this is the happy life, to rejoice to thee, of thee, for thee; this it is, and there is no other.

It is so, precisely because, as St. Thomas Aquinas said, "God alone satisfies." This is precisely what Jesus is conveying in the parable of the rich man whose land produced so abundantly that he didn't know what to do with the crops.

Then he said, "I will do this: I will pull down my barns and build larger ones, and there I will store all my grain and my goods. And I will say to my soul, 'Soul, you have ample goods laid up for many years; relax, eat, drink, be merry.'" But God said to him, "You fool! This very night your life is being demanded of you. And the things you have prepared, whose will they be?" So it is with those who store up treasures for themselves but are not rich toward God. (Lk 12:18–21)

Jesus' joy is beyond material gain, social contentment, and fortunate circumstances. God wants us to savor the heavenly joy by surrendering totally to the divine will.

Such a beatific experience that makes us "participants of the divine nature" (2 Pet 1:4) "teaches us," as the *Catechism of the Catholic Church* states, "that true happiness is not found in riches or well-being, in human fame or power, or in any human achievement—however beneficial it may be—such as science, technology, and art, or indeed in any creature, but in God alone, the source of every good and of all love" (1723).

Radical Optimism

In our world today, we have undeniable reasons for tears and depression. But when we look at reality in a deeper way, we will discover that laughter is not only the appropriate response, but also a truer response to life than tears and depression. No matter how much we are able to laugh, we do not laugh enough. Things may be ridiculous, surprising, funny, or unexpected, but there is a more profound reason for laughter: closeness to God. A joy like this has the characteristics of truth, presence, creativity, humility, surrender, and love.

How can we be sad when we realize the truth of being God's children? How can we hide our excitement when we know that God is present at all times, in all things, in all circumstance of our lives? How can we hold back celebrations of the fruits of our actions when we become aware of the fact that it is our Creator who gave us the gift of cocreating? How can we fail to be delighted and inflamed with ecstasy when we know that we cannot do anything by ourselves—which should makes us humble—but we can do everything through Jesus Christ (see Jn 15:5; Phil 4:13)? How can we fail to enjoy understanding the divine mystery if we love God and God's creation? How can we fail to have a radical optimism when we believe that the Holy Spirit speaks in our lives and in the circumstances and times in which we live?

Pope John XXIII was a good example of such optimism. Reading his journal, one cannot help noticing the continual growth of trust in the providence of God, and the discernment of God's voice in the events of his time. When he called for the Second Vatican Council, he certainly was aware of the difficulties and hard work it would demand, especially at his age of eighty-one. But he trusted God's plan. For him, the calling of the Council was one of the "great graces bestowed on a man who has a low esteem of himself but receives good inspiration and humbly and trustfully proceeds to put it into practice."

How can a work fail if it is the fruit of God's inspiration? How can we fail to be optimistic if we follow God's way? God has a plan for the world and for each and every one of us. From this angle, pessimism seems completely unrealistic and inappropriate. Religious people, according to recent studies conducted in several universities, cope better with crises than nonreligious people, and they are less depressed, less anxious, and less suicidal. Religion provides, among other benefits, a spiritual and social support, as well as a sense of purpose and meaning in life. Beware of a joyless religion. Joyless Christians do not worship God, but their own "virtue" and "righteousness." "Christians," as it has been rightly said, "should look more redeemed."

Ultimately, by saying "yes" to existence, we express gratitude and joy to God, and we define our true selves whose radical optimism is evident because of the realization that we are of God's delights. Julian of Norwich says, "And what can make us rejoice more in God than to see in him that in us, of all his greatest works, he has joy?"

We can be God's joy as God is our joy only if we become "a new creation," as Paul says, "so if anyone is in Christ, there is a new creation: everything old has passed away; see, everything has become new" (2 Cor 5:17). This "new creation" is the fruit of a new consciousness that is God's gift of unconditional and eternal love for us. Love invokes communion.

Communion suggests oneness—the oneness that is more than the consent of hearts, minds, and will, but, as Thomas Merton put it, "a mystical union in which Christ himself becomes the source and principle of divine life in me." Oneness with God makes the saint a person of joy. He or she embraces the present moment, joining the divine dance and blossoming like the almond tree that Greek novelist Nikos Kazantzakis observed: "I said to the almond tree: 'Speak to me of God.' And the almond tree blossomed."

Religious people are the happiest people.

Holiness: A Blossoming Life

Joy grows or diminishes according to how close to or far from God we are. Saints are supposed to be joyful persons, precisely because of this closeness to God. They preach the good news through words, through their living example, and especially through both together. The deep joy they radiate comes from their closeness to God. Their joy is evidence of their sanctity. According to Mother Teresa, people discover God in the joy shown by others. She said:

The world today is hungering for the joy that

comes from a pure heart, because the pure heart sees God…. A smile costs little but it does so much good…. Joy shines forth in the eyes and the glance, in one's conversation and in the expression of one's countenance. When people see the happiness in your eyes, they will discover God within you.

God's strong presence in the saints gives them a joy that is quite different from how our culture sees joy—absence of illness, persecution, disappointment, and failure. Many saints, starting with St. Paul, had reasons to be unhappy, but they were happy anyway. God's gift of joy was by far stronger than the miseries to which they were subjected. Joy allowed them to see something bigger than the daily circumstances of their lives; it gave them a different perspective on reality. After all, a true Christian cannot help but have an eschatological view that results in the triumph of good and eternal joy. G. K. Chesterton observed: "Great joy does not gather the rose buds while it may; its eyes are fixed on the immortal rose which Dante saw. Great joy has in it the sense of immortality."

Many Christians, however, do not seem to live joyful lives. The indwelling presence of the Trinity's community of love in them remains only an intellectual idea that hasn't touched their daily existence. They are not able to realize the all-ness of God in their lives. They misinterpret the very message of Christianity, which is "good news of great joy" (Lk 2:10). They miss the true consequence of the Incarnation and the Resurrection, which is to be Alleluia people. They underestimate the value of childlike abandonment to God; and cannot understand that they have to "live by the Spirit" (Gal 5:16) so that they can enjoy "newness of life" (Rom 6:4). Many Christians do not know that joy adds depth to everything they do. They don't know how to both communicate, and "be" a message of joy. Saints succeed in this endeavor. For them, the "good news" is received not as knowledge, but as a reality in the present moment—here and now—and they are transformed. The perceptible speaks for the imperceptible.

Saints see an intrinsic link between holiness and joy. St. Ignatius recommended that his followers "laugh, and grow strong." St. Teresa of Avila prayed, "From sour-faced saints, O Lord, deliver us." St. Francis said, "Let the brothers ever avoid appearing gloomy, sad, and clouded, like the hypocrites; but let one ever be found joyous in the Lord, gay, amiable, gracious, as is meet." St. Francis de Sales said, "A sad saint is a sorry saint."

The truth is that joy is not only the byproduct of a holy life, but it can also help to produce a holy life because "the joy of the Lord is your strength" (Neh 8:10). It is easier to overcome sin when one has hope and joy in God; the joy of the holy is by far more satisfying than the passing pleasures of sin.

"From sour-faced saints, O Lord, deliver us." — St. Teresa of Avila

By living the fullness of Christian life, saints transform reality. Holiness does not leave things the way they are. In the documents of the Second Vatican Council, we read the following: "It is evident to everyone that all the faithful of Christ of whatever rank or status are called to the fullness of the Christian life and to the perfection of charity. By this holiness a more human way of life is promoted even in this earthly society" (*Lumen Gentium*, 40). It is so because God speaks to us through these saints. The Council continues:

For when we look at the lives of those who have faithfully followed Christ, we are inspired with a new reason for seeking the city which is to come (Heb 13:14; 11:10). At the same time we are shown a most safe path by which, among the vicissitudes of this world and in keeping with the state in life and condition proper to each of us, we will be able to arrive at perfect union with Christ, that is, holiness. In the lives of those who shared in our humanity and yet were transformed into especially successful images of Christ (cf. 2 Cor 3:18), God vividly manifests His presence and His face. He speaks to us in them, and gives us a sign of His kingdom, to which we are powerfully drawn, surrounded as we are by so many witnesses (cf. Heb 12:1), and having such an argument for the truth of the gospel. (*Lumen Gentium*, 50)

God's joy is our strength. It supersedes frustrations, discouragement, and the various types of disappointments we encounter in life. Also, it sets the right relationship with God, others, and ourselves. Deep joy comes when we encounter God in the ordinary, the mystery, and the profound. To know joy is to know God and to pray "thy will be done" at all times and under all circumstances. In due time you will marvel at God's consistent care of you, and your joy will be complete and will never cease.

FOR YOUR REFLECTION & RESPONSE

1. What is most important in your life? Have you ever made a list of your priorities? What are they for you? Are you doing the things that give your life meaning? If not, what is preventing you from doing so?

2. Because desire caused the fall of Adam and Eve, do you think it is possible that human desire is an obstacle to happiness? Does personal desire contradict God's will and goodness? But then where does this desire for happiness come from if not from God? Where, in your opinion, can happiness be found?

3. People of great joy cannot be offended because they know who they are. How can Jesus, for example, be offended? If you know exactly who you are, why would anything offend you? Do you feel this way? If not, why not?

4. List three things from your everyday life that bring you joy. How do these things affect your relationship with God? How would you like to express your love and gratitude to God? How can you actively express this love, for example, as the psalmists did?

5. How do you usually react to discomfort? Do you often use, at least unconsciously, the words, "If only"? (For example: if only I did not have this crisis, I would have been happy; if only I had this or that, I would have been happy, etc.) Rather than thinking "if only," what practical steps do you take when you are dissatisfied with your life? What would you change if you knew that every act is a healing prayer for yourself and for everyone around you?

AFFIRMATION

Repeat this several times a day.

I celebrate my closeness to God today and everyday.

Prayer

Dear God,

You are the God of joy and celebration.

You are the God of love and peace.

You have made us to "rejoice and be glad" (Ps 118:24); make me live this way, today and all days.

Keep my hope as fresh as morning, my enthusiasm as invigorating as determination, and my cheers as gregarious as a playful child. In any way and in all ways, grant me the grace to radiate your presence—the fullness of joy—for "in your presence there is fullness of joy" (Ps 16:11).

Make of my life an instrument for spreading your joy to all those who are around me. Make me the image of your enfolding presence in the world.

Let my joy be complete—a joy without ceasing. Amen.

CHAPTER THREE

The Power of Joy

"A cheerful heart is good medicine."

■ PROVERBS 17:22

Inner joy is power. The better you feel, the better you are. The better you are, the better you are able to do. Then, your spirit is higher, your heart is more involved, and your mind is more creative. Also, your enthusiasm for living becomes more noticeable and your horizons expand. If you take a moment to reflect on yourself, you will realize that your new perception is telling you something. What is it?

45

One of the tragedies of our human condition is that we use only ten percent of our strength and potential. The poet Victor Hugo (1802–1885) observed: "People don't lack strength, they lack will."

Our dormant capacities can and should be awakened, and this can be done through inner joy. Inner joy gives us energy, enthusiasm, zest for living, courage, confidence, and creativity.

Have you noticed the change in your own life or the life of a loved one when one's full potential is used instead of ten percent? Have you noticed the inner shift from a negative attitude to positive transformation and optimism? This shift is not a shallow change of moods. It is deep in the person's psyche, and it is heavy with consequences.

When perception changes, reality itself changes. It has to. A lower level of consciousness corresponds to a lower level of spiritual, emotional, and physical discontent, dis-quiet, and dis-ease. A higher level of consciousness corresponds to a higher level of healthy interaction and general well-being.

With a well-adjusted perception, you will shift your "I'll be happy when…" into "I'm happy now, no matter what." You will start to feel good about yourself, love yourself, and take care of yourself. You will accomplish more because you feel satisfied with your work. You will nurture genuine relationships with others based on true love, respect, and justice. You will learn to listen more to your inner voice and fundamental purpose in life, which is imprinted by God in your soul. Then you will see your resentments, hidden anger, and disappointments vanish—as futile things often do.

The healing process consists first and foremost in changing your inner vision. In his way, Marcel Proust put it well when he said, "The real voyage of discovery consists not in seeking new landscapes but in having new eyes."

I am not sure about the theory of those who believe that the human condition is essentially and intrinsically unhappy. The real problem, as I see it, is not "out there." It is within—in the way we see the problem. We have the power to create our lives joyfully. Inner joy is a formidable force. It is so because it is the fruit of being who we are.

In a sense, inner joy is a counter-cultural virtue. What you are saying when you practice this virtue is, "This is me. This is what I have to offer. This is what I am supposed to be. This is what makes me special and unique." Affirming your individuality separates you from those who expect you to conform to their expectations. The poet e.e. cummings (1894–1962) puts it this way:

> To be nobody but yourself in a world that is doing its best, night and day to make you like everybody else, means to fight the hardest battle which any human being can fight, and never stop fighting.

As many psychological studies have shown, most people would rather conform, follow the crowd, and not take the risk of rejection. But the truth of the matter is that only when you are yourself can you realize your potential, be the best you can be, and discover the capacity for inner joy that transforms everything and makes you reach the fullness of life. This is exactly what St. Paul was trying to convey to the Romans when he wrote, "Do not be conformed to the world. But be transformed by the renewing of your minds, so that you may discern what is the will of God—what is good and acceptable and perfect" (Rom 12:2). Conformity to others' expectations does not give you joy. Conformity to God's will for you—this is what you really are—gives you transforming and healing joy, so longed for in the depth of your heart.

Dolores Heart was a blue-eyed blonde, a movie star

with many films already to her credit, including *Loving You* costarring Elvis Presley. Why, at twenty-four, did this young woman, who seemed to have everything going her way, quit Hollywood fame to enter an abbey in Bethlehem, Connecticut? Why would anyone give up a star's crown for a nun's black hood and white collar? Why would anyone leave behind wealth, pleasure, and power to become an austere Benedictine nun who chants Latin prayers eight times a day starting at 1:50 AM and who performs ordinary tasks in the garden and kitchen? If you ask this woman, who is now sixty-seven, the Rev. Mother Dolores Hart, prioress of Regina Laudis (Queen of Praise) in Bethlehem, Connecticut, she will tell you:

> I came to understand that God truly expressed himself through his beloved. And through a mystery of great love, he broke through the extravagance of the motion picture industry to make my vocation known to me.

She also said: "Fall in love with life. A nun must become a lover in a new way she never expects. A vocation is a marriage with Christ."

Dolores Hart is a striking, living example of the journey toward inner joy. Her unusual story was among

Inner joy is truly a gift from God.

those in an exhibit titled "God's Women: Nuns in America" that took place at the Pope John Paul II Cultural Center in Washington, DC, in 2004. Three American women who became saints, Elizabeth Ann Seton, Frances Cabrini, and Katharine Drexel, were also featured. The chief operating officer at the Center said: "The overreaching theme of the exhibit is one of joy, particularly the joy these women have in their vocations—in their impact on this country and its culture."

In order to be able to reach authentic joy, a renewing of the mind—a new perception and new birth—is required. Here is the solution, but also the problem. Erich Fromm observed, "Living is the process of continuous rebirth. The tragedy is that we die before we are fully born."

How many of us are able to reach this extraordinary inner joy? We long for it. We strive for it. We stretch our arms to grasp it. But we know that it is one of the fruits of the Holy Spirit (see Gal 5:22) and a gift from God.

Inner Joy

There is a hidden agenda—a conspiracy—in the world today. At its core is the belief that "what works for us, the producers, should work for you, the consumers." This belief is generally led by economists, social planners, politicians, and all those who convince you that if you want to be happy you should buy their products.

Please, wake up! Believe only what is in tune with the real longing of your soul—what makes you healthy, happy, and holy. Deep joy will not come from outside you. It lies within you. Your inner joy—if authentic—does not turn you from others, but toward them. Inner joy makes you trust yourself and leads you naturally to a new and genuine sense of community. Inner joy does not allow you to sit back and distance yourself from social problems. You want your inner values to be shared and spread. When shared, this kind of joy, paradoxically, grows. Your fulfilled longings make you enthusiastic for life, wanting to live it to the fullest possible. Committed to your own growth in the path designed by God for you, you will not have any time left for complaints, gloomy forecasts, and pessimism. When problems arise, God's grace will help you solve them and move on.

By changing yourself, you change the world. Changing the world is, then, the result of changing yourself. You start first. Socrates, long ago, revealed this secret, "Let him who would move the world first move himself." The ideal society would emerge only from healthy and fully developed individuals. The philosopher Bertrand Russell (1872–1970) observed:

> When I allow myself to hope that the world will emerge from its present troubles, I see before me a shining vision: a world where work is pleasant and not excessive, where kindly feelings are common, where minds released from fear create delight for eye, ear, and heart. Do not say this is impossible. It is not impossible if people would bend their minds to the achievement of the kind of happiness that should be distinctive of man.

Inner joy is a favored tool for personal and social healing and transformation because of its deep connection with love. It can be considered another name for or another way to look at love. This connection adds a critical element to the healing power of joy.

The Joy Prescription

Ancient wisdom defines the universe, and particularly all living things, as being more than a sum of their parts, and it points to the necessity and importance of integration and interaction. Therefore, when we talk about a healthy human being, we mean the healthy interaction and integration of the physical, mental, emotional, spiritual, and ecological components. Again, Socrates has something to say here: "As it is not proper to cure the eyes without the head, nor the head without the body, so neither is it proper to cure the body without the soul." Certain equilibrium is required in order to reach this needed well-being.

We have joy when our life is meaningful.

But, how to get there from here? You might want to consider the following points.

Live a meaningful life. How does joy, whose roots go much deeper than those of happiness, come to us? Author and psychologist Victor E. Frankl (1905–1997) offered this answer: "Joy comes into our lives when we have (a) something to do, (b) someone to love, and (c) something to hope for." In other words, we have joy when our life is meaningful.

Find your purpose in life. Do you have a mission statement? If not, write one. When you know what your life is all about, you will know what is really important to you and what is not. And this is also how you get more out of your life.

Live your dream. Joy is not felt when you live someone else's dream. It is your own dream that gives you reason to wake up in the morning and do what you have to do. Joy is a choice—your choice. It gives meaning to the rest of the day and the rest of your life.

Some people tell you how to be happy. Others sell you products that supposedly make you happy, and they bombard you with their versions of happiness. But is their conception of happiness yours? People of joy may listen to different opinions, but they know how to look deeply within themselves to envision what is right for them and what gives them the joy they want. Joseph Campbell, when he appeared on Bill Moyer's television documentary "The Power of Myth," said: "If you follow your bliss, you put yourself on a kind of track that has been there the whole while, waiting for you, and the life that you ought to be living is the one you are living." Take time to rightly develop the discerning ability to listen to your inner voice.

Live in the present moment. Do not be a worrier. Learn from the past and hope for a great future, but live only in the here and now. This is God's will for you. Jean-Pierre de Caussade, S.J. (1675–1751) wrote in his book *Abandonment to Divine Providence*: "The secret of sanctity consists in but one thing, fidelity to God's will as it is manifested in the duties of the present moment." Joy is now; worry is past and future.

Laugh as often as you can. Laughter has an important

role when a reduction of tension and stress is needed. When the muscles are in a state of deep relaxation, being anxious becomes more difficult. In their research, William F. Fay Jr., M.D., emeritus professor of clinical psychiatry at Stanford University, and Lee Berk Stanley Tan of Lama Linda University, California, came to the conclusion that "mirthful laughter" has good benefits for the body. It can strengthen the immune system, reduce the level of stress and pain, stimulate blood circulation, breathing, and mental functions, and improve muscle tone. This was the idea behind the creation of laughing clubs. The first of these clubs was founded in India, in March 1995, and its credo was "Laugh louder and live longer." For Dr. Madan Kataria, the founder of Laughter Clubs International, laughter can lower blood pressure, boost the immune system, reduce stress, give energy, and provide general well-being of the body, mind, and soul.

The story of author and *Saturday Review* editor Norman Cousins reminds us of the accuracy and suitability of this theory. Indeed, Cousins claimed that he laughed away a life-threatening form of arthritis. This

> Laughter can add years to your life while adding life to your years.

also gives reason to believe what satirist Jonathan Swift (1667–1745) said: "The best doctors in the world are Dr. Diet, Dr. Quiet, and Dr. Merryman." Laughing certainly matters. It can add years to your life while adding life to your years. You can make the world happier and healthier one laugh at a time.

Meet your spiritual needs. Knowing it or not, we do have a God instinct, and this is essential to our well-being. To pretend that God does not exist or that God has nothing to do with us will sooner or later contribute to our misery. God makes your life meaningful because of his purpose for your life. If you lose the very meaning of your life, everything becomes trivial, dull, and boring, and you lose your inner joy. Then, deterioration in your general well-being is bound to happen.

Everyone should find the authentic spiritual nurturing that speaks to his or her heart and mind and that can be integrated into his or her daily existence. This is an essential component of inner healing joy. Beatrice Bruteau, author and founder of the Schola Contemplationis in North Carolina, wrote:

> I think most of the spiritual life is really a matter of relaxing…. Once the water is calm, it also becomes transparent. Then you can look down through it, clear to the bottom. When our mind

becomes clear and transparent, we can perceive what lies at its bottom, its foundation: it is the peace of God, the divine Eternity. Then the mind rests happily in this state, even while we go about our business, doing the things that need to be done.

Moreover, we read in Isaiah: "All who keep the Sabbath, and do not profane it, and hold fast my covenant—these I will bring to my holy mountain, and make them joyful in my house of prayer" (Isa 56:6–7).

Integrate spiritual life in your search for true happiness. To every human being's life, there is undoubtedly a contemplative dimension because everyone, sooner or later, will have to face fundamental questions such as life and death, identity and relationships to God and to others. One need not necessarily be a person of great piety to have to answer these questions. When your moment of truth arrives, you will discover that these questions were your own too.

Seek balance. Look at the people around you. The happiest are those who are the most balanced. They always have a certain positive energy that radiates from them. They have found in their lives the point of wise moderation and equilibrium. They do not have to prove their success. They have what they have because it is well-deserved. They are who and what they are. They are more balanced because they are more centered. This is what balance mainly does: it helps the person center physically, psychologically, and spiritually.

Know yourself. Joy is not just a feeling of euphoria. Think of joy as the result of learning who you really are, what you are meant to do, and do it as something you love. When we envision and experience a sense of direction about ourselves, we feel good. Our fundamental purpose in life is not only in our best interest, but it is also an important ingredient of our inner joy and general well-being. You are not your job. You are not what you possess. You are not your nationality. When you drop all this, you still exist. Knowing the very essence of your existence will delight you and contribute greatly to your healing and growth.

Simplify. Life is becoming more and more complicated and increasingly chaotic. Technology changes rapidly and so does the understanding of our values. Concepts such as "moral," "normal," and "acceptable," for example, have been redefined and revised many times. Clutter at every level—physically, emotionally, intellectually, and even spiritually—is becoming part of our daily life. It's time to simplify. It's time to sort what is important and what is not. It's time to be straightforward and honest with ourselves and others. "Blessed are the simple," wrote Thomas à Kempis in *The Imitation of Christ*, "for they shall have much peace" and joy. Also, remember the advice of Henry David Thoreau (1817–1862),

> Give joy and it will be given back to you.

> Simplicity, Simplicity, Simplicity! I say, let your affairs be as two or three, and not a hundred or a thousand; instead of a million count half a dozen, and keep your accounts on your thumbnail.…Simplify, simplify.

Remember also the words of Winston Churchill: "All great things are simple."

Share your joy. Joy is one of those gifts that when given away, comes back to you multiplied. It fits so snugly into Jesus' command, "Give, and it will be given to you" (Lk 6:38), that it can be inserted into it. If one day you are lonely, befriend someone; if you feel sadness, give happiness; if you are troubled by something, comfort someone; and see the difference this makes to you.

Joy, when given away and shared with others, comes back to you multiplied. It benefits everyone involved. Mother Teresa saw the importance of joy for her sisters' mission. She would tell them:

Joy is a need and a power for us, even physically. A Sister who has cultivated a spirit of joy feels less tired and is always ready to go [on] doing good. A Sister filled with joy preaches without preaching. A joyful Sister is like the sunshine of God's love, the hope of eternal happiness, the flame of burning love.

Also: "Let no one ever come to you without coming away better and happier."

Moreover, joy will never run out. There's plenty of it to go around. One of its mysteries is that when you give it away it grows within you. It flows and flows and flows. It is like the story of Elijah who asked the widow to give him her last piece of bread. "The jar of meal was not emptied, neither did the jug of oil fail, according to the word of the Lord that he spoke by Elijah" (1 Kings 17:16).

Be good to yourself. St. Paul sees the body as the temple of the Holy Spirit (see 1 Cor 6:19). Therefore, taking care of your body should be a physical and spiritual duty. Exercise, diet, and all that contribute to better health affect your spiritual life, too. Your good health stimulates your joy. Your joy stimulates your good health. Centuries ago, it was already known that "a cheerful heart is good medicine, but a downcast spirit dries up the bones" (Prov 17:22). But, joy does not come in such ready forms—liquid, pill, or capsule. It may take a good amount of time, effort, and determination.

Transform your outlook. When you have negative emotions, replace them with positive ones. In *The Art of Happiness,* the Dalai Lama said: "I think that cultivating positive mental states like kindness and compassion definitely leads to better psychological health and happiness." Then he added: "Achieving genuine happiness may require bringing about a transformation in your outlook, your way of thinking, and this is not a simple matter." Your perception creates your reality. Make sure that you have untainted lenses.

Free yourself from the ego. The ego, which is the false self that we make up, has the capacity to define, interpret, and judge. It also controls and manipulates. In this sense, it can be a tyrant and you don't know it. There is no possible joy in an ego-driven mind.

Love fully. By extending compassion and empathy everywhere to everyone, the pain of life will diminish considerably, as Sophocles (496–406 BC) suggested, "One word frees us all of the weight and pain of life. That word is love," and also Euripides (480–406 BC), "Love is all we have, the only way that each can help the other." People who have joy in their hearts are involved, responsive, attentive, appreciative, and dedicated.

How lovely it is to wish each other a "Happy New Year!" But the fact is that a new year will never be happy unless we are happy. The sun will rise and set nevertheless; the day will come and go; events will occur and vanish. This next year will not be different from the preceding ones unless we awaken to our full potential and enjoy our new selves. Happy new selves make for a happy new year, and happy, healthy, and holy lives.

FOR YOUR REFLECTION & RESPONSE

1. Are you living and maintaining a healthy lifestyle? Are faith, hope, and love important to you? Do they help you in extending compassion and empathy to others? Do you make your life "something beautiful for God," as Mother Teresa would say?

2. Do you do things with enthusiasm? Why or why not? Do you surround yourself with things that inspire beauty, harmony, and order, and a sense of wonder and gratitude? How do you find joy in the complexity and stress of daily life? What makes you really happy?

3. Here are three situations in which you might be involved at the present time or in the future. Write down what you might do about them.

(a) A friend of yours is stuck in a bad situation that you know will get worse day by day. (b) You are wrongly accused by a coworker or by your boss of doing something dishonest. (c) You know that you need a particular skill in order to follow your purpose in life, but you have neither money nor time to pursue it.

The following questions might help you in your answers. "Am I able to see things from someone else's perspective?" "Do I have the courage to imagine things differently?" "Can I discipline myself to make the needed changes?"

4. Consciously or unconsciously, how do you feel you are living your life—in the present, in

the past, or in the future? What motivates you—your true self or your ego—to make changes in your life? What are the attitudes and behaviors you might have that are preventing you from being healthy, happy, and holy?

5. What goals have you achieved that give you great joy? Do you have other goals that you have done nothing about? Do you feel that your life is what you really want it to be? What are you willing to sacrifice in order to be who you really are—the person designed by God, to be happy, healthy, and holy?

AFFIRMATION

Repeat this several times a day.

No one can rob me of my joy today, but I choose to give it away.

Prayer

Dear God,

There is so much in this world that brings tears to our eyes. But there is much more that makes us laugh in delight and deep joy.

May our tears and laughter deepen our faith in you and reflect your unconditional love and care for your creation.

Make us understand you in tears and laughter and, with the accuracy human beings are capable of, reflect your everlasting joy.

In your image you have created us. Are you hurt when we fail to reflect your image? Are you sad when we do not see you in others? Are you angry when we worship other gods? Are you able to keep the feast on when we ask you to "give [us] the share of the property that will belong to [us]" (Lk 15:12) and go away from you?

Grant us the gift of joy so we can see in our laughter the beauty of your bounty and in our wounds the windows to your infinite goodness and the urgency of a new life. Amen.

Joy is not about accumulating wealth, obtaining power, or indulging in pleasures. It is about living the fullness of life while achieving the optimum emotional, psychological, and spiritual balance. Why should the accumulation of external things make sense when joy stems from within? Are you getting what you want from them? Is "yes" the correct answer of our consumption society to such questions?

That hole of dissatisfaction and emptiness undermines the moments of happiness we may experience from time to time. And that is good because our continuous quest for more and more happiness demonstrates the need for perfection, immensity, and eternity—God, the infinite joy—even though we often do not know that it is God we are searching for. God is hidden behind the fleeting moment of happiness, but we do not know it, which is the reason joy seems to always have a taste of the unattainable. It is why happiness is a journey in time and in depth—a new way of seeing oneself in relationship with God and the world.

When we truly see ourselves as children of God and acknowledge God's infinite love for us, we cannot but live in the delight that honors the giver of life. "The greatest honor you can give to God," observed mystic Julian of Norwich (1342–1416), "is to live gladly, joyfully because of the knowledge of his love." Only then, and no matter what our circumstances are, "Those who wish to sing always find a song," as a Swedish proverb puts it, and they do it with all their heart, might, and exaltation.

When joy becomes our deepest connection with God—the very ground of our true self—it will give us a sense of inner balance and poise, which is a necessary ingredient in the process of healing our body and soul.

When we learn to see life, not with our eyes, but with God's eyes, even helplessness can become a state of grace, and wounds can become windows and pathways to God. Then, life is just wonders, blessings, and bliss because God is life. Then, a genuine smile says that God is in control and that God's joy heals the most somber and gloomy faces. There is no such thing as terminal "sadness" when our smile is the fruit of deep faith.

Are you getting what you want and the satisfaction you are looking for in your life? Before answering this question, remember that you can be more than what you have been, and that no matter where you go, you cannot get away from your true self. Do not try to run away from yourself; you cannot. Rather, go deeper in yourself, further and further, until you discover the riches and treasures of God's grace.

Joy is not only about setting things right in your life, but also and especially about seeing things rightly—with the mind of Christ (see 1 Cor 2:14–16). God's glory is our joyful gratitude for our blessings. Joy is a living thanksgiving prayer.